Salads in Jars Cookbook

Healthy, Quick and Easy Mason Jar Recipes

Louise Davidson

Copyrights

All rights reserved © Louise Davidson and The Cookbook Publisher. No part of this publication or the information in it may be quoted from or reproduced in any form by means such as printing, scanning, photocopying, or otherwise without prior written permission of the copyright holder.

Disclaimer and Terms of Use

Effort has been made to ensure that the information in this book is accurate and complete. However, the author and the publisher do not warrant the accuracy of the information, text, and graphics contained within the book due to the rapidly changing nature of science, research, known and unknown facts, and internet. The author and the publisher do not hold any responsibility for errors, omissions, or contrary interpretation of the subject matter herein. This book is presented solely for motivational and informational purposes only.

The recipes provided in this book are for informational purposes only and are not intended to provide dietary advice. A medical practitioner should be consulted before making any changes in diet. Additionally, recipe cooking times may require adjustment depending on age and quality of appliances. Readers are strongly urged to take all precautions to ensure ingredients are fully cooked in order to avoid the dangers of foodborne illnesses. The recipes and suggestions provided in this book are solely the opinion of the author. The author and publisher do not take any responsibility for any consequences that may result due to following the instructions provided in this book.

ISBN: 978-1533081407

Printed in the United States

Avant-Propos

Mason jars are familiar to everyone. They've been around forever, filling up the back of our cupboards and shelves in garages alike. These traditional canning jars seem to be the most unlikely candidate to take the internet by storm. But they are now being embraced by food bloggers, health enthusiasts, and event planners, among a whole host of unlikely candidates. The humble mason jar's function has been rapidly redefined beyond its traditional role in preserving, canning, and pickling fruits and vegetables. From drinking jars to candle holders, the mason jar is becoming more versatile and it is an outlet for expressing creative ideas.

One of the most popular new purposes for the jar is to use it as a container for packing salads. Aesthetically, the bright and cheerful layers of rainbow-colored vegetables is a mood booster, and they make healthy food look cool as a cucumber. But beyond looks, the jar salads also present practical options for packing and transporting salads to work. The tall vertical design of the jars means salad ingredients need to be stacked on top of each other. This forces the separation of the dressing from the delicate ingredients, helping to preserve the freshness and crispness of the greens.

It is because of this convenience and practicality that packing salads in jars seems likely to stick around for a long while. And the beauty of these jar meals is that the possibilities are endless when creating your own salad. This book introduces the basic layering technique to ensure that the salad stays in optimum condition. The 50 recipes here suggest various ingredient combinations that you can experiment with. But do not be constrained by them, and take the liberty of substituting with your favorite ingredients, such as eggs, avocado, and bacon. Make them as hearty or as light as you like and they will be your next favorite work lunch option!

Contents

Introduction 1
  Tips for Preparing and Packing Salads in Jars 3
  Types of Jars to Use 7
Recipes 9
  Chicken and Spinach Salad 9
  Buffalo Chicken Salad 11
  Italian Antipasto Salad 30
  Bacon and Egg Avocado Salad 13
  Spinach with Strawberries and Bacon Salad 15
  Creamy Broccoli and Ham Salad 17
  Roast Beef and Potato Salad 19
  Thai Beef Noodle Salad Jar 21
  Minty Turkey and Chickpea Salad 23
  Ground Turkey Taco Salad 25
  Shrimp Feta Cobb Salad with Ranch Dressing 27
  Peppery Egg and Tuna Salad 29
  Prawn, Rice and Mango Salad 30
  Smoked Salmon and Sugar Snap Pea Salad 31
  Ginger Miso Salmon Salad 33
  Zucchini Quinoa Salad with Avocado Lime Dressing 35
  Classic Greek salad 37
  Refreshing Caprese Salad in a Jar 39
  Black Bean and Corn Salad 41
  Sweet Potato Salad 43
  Chickpea Salad with Mint Yogurt Dressing 45
  Crunchy Green Bean and Feta Salad 47
  Rainbow Avocado Salad with Citrus Dressing 49
  Tofu and Bell Pepper Salad 51
  Red Pesto Zucchini Noodle Salad 53
  Pomegranate and Pear Feta Salad 55
  Rainbow Fruit Salad 56
  Camembert Grape Salad with Honey Vinaigrette 57

Spinach, Blueberry and Blue Cheese Salad..............58
Strawberry Goat Cheese Salad 59
Lemon Pesto Pasta Salad in a Jar 61
Chicken and Orzo Salad with Creamy Citrus Dressing 63
Spinach, Snap Peas, and Orzo Salad 65
Sundried Tomato Pesto and Salami Pasta Salad......67
Creamy Chicken Caesar Pasta Salad 69
Spinach and Fresh Mozzarella Pasta Salad..............71
Pearl Couscous and Roasted Beetroot Salad 73
Italian Tortellini Salad 75
Kale and Arugula Citrus Couscous Salad..................77
Ranch Chicken Pasta Salad 79
Farro and Chickpea salad..81
Farro, Cabbage and Apple Salad 83
Quinoa-Chia Curry Salad...85
Quinoa Burrito Bowl Salad...87
Roasted Sweet Potato with Quinoa Salad.................89
Tabbouleh Quinoa Salad 91
Barley and Kale Salad 93
Barley, Feta, and Asparagus Salad 95
Apple and Orange Buckwheat Salad.........................97
Mediterranean Millet Salad 99
About the Author 101
More Books from Louise Davidson..........................102
Appendix - Cooking Conversion Charts.....................105

Introduction

Lunch at work can be boring. You might have exhausted all the dining options around your office. Or you might be tired of the regular sandwich and wraps repertoire in your brown bag lunches. Why not jazz up your midday meal with a healthier option that can be made in a cinch and is also stunning to look at?

Yes, we are talking about salads in a jar. You might already have seen these salads in a jar on Pinterest or Facebook because they are ubiquitous across the blogosphere. These layered salads make a bold and bright statement that will easily make you the envy of your colleagues in the office. Instead of reaching out for another sandwich stuffed with bacon and oozy cheese, this book is here to help inspire you to create hearty salads that are packed with fresh leafy greens, sweet zesty fruits and bits of your favourite nuts, cheese, and bacon.

Before scoffing at packing meals in a jar as a passing food fad that champions style over substance, think again. One of the many reasons for its popularity is due to its practicality. By layering the salad ingredients in a particular order, and taking advantage of the tall vertical design of canning jars, we keep the wet dressing separated from the delicate ingredients. This provides a convenient solution to transporting the salad and dressing all in one container but keeping the delicate salad leaves fresh and crunchy.

These jar meals make great pack-and-carry options that you can easily reach for inside the fridge when you run out the door in the morning. Gone are those days when you realize that you have forgotten to take your dressing container together with your salad.

The only equipment you need for these meals are regular canning jars, which are probably sitting somewhere in the kitchen pantry. For those environmentally conscious, these jars are sustainable packaging that can be re-used for years if they are well taken care of. They are spill-proof, which means no more messy dressing leakages when transporting them, and more crucially, they are airtight so the greens to last for a longer period of time.

Another benefit of these salad jar meals is that they can be prepared and assembled during the weekends to ensure a healthy supply of food for the week ahead. Doing so not only saves time and effort, but also helps with portion control. Furthermore, planning ahead also makes for good budgeting because you can be more conscious of your expenditure.

This book recognises the immense potential of jar meals by presenting 50 different creations that will hopefully motivate you to put together your own healthy masterpiece. The recipes will cover salads that contain meat, seafood, vegetables only, fruits, pasta, and grains. They can be easily customized based on individual and portion preferences. Give them a try because the possibilities are endless!

Tips for Preparing and Packing Salads in Jars

Salads are meals that can be made ahead of time, and the freshness of the greens is better extended because the canning jars are airtight. If you are intending to get them ready in advance, here are some tips and tricks to help you prepare salad jar meals more efficiently but ensure that there is still lots of variety in your meals.

Wash and pat dry your vegetables and fruits
No one wants to eat slimy and wilted vegetables. After washing them, always use a salad spinner or manually pat them dry and leave them out on a baking sheet to air dry for a short while. For vegetables and fruits that are wetter, such as tomatoes and cucumbers, consider removing their wet bits before adding them into the jar. Otherwise, if you do not mind them soaking up more dressing, simply place them right inside the dressing, which will effectively pickle them.

Chop your food up into smaller pieces
In order to fit into a canning jar, greens that have been washed and patted dry need to be in cut into smaller pieces than when serving them in a bowl. Make sure hardier vegetables such as romaine lettuce are chopped up in small chunks so that they can fit into the jar and take up less space. Also tear up the delicate greens such as spinach and arugula to make sure that they are in bite-sized pieces for easy eating.

Prepare a variety of toppings to mix and match
If you are one of those who much prefer sandwiches with bacon and oozy eggs, salads might be an option of last resort for you. To make it more appealing, avoid repeating the same combination every day by changing up the toppings. You might want to have on hand precooked hardboiled eggs, dried fruits or nuts, leftover roast beef, or anything else that catches your fancy. When you are ready to bring them to work, just stick them into your jar and you will always have a different meal for the day

To pack salads inside canning jars, the key to preventing sad and limp greens is to layer the different layers correctly. Once you have mastered the basic concept, you are on your way to creating hundreds and thousands of different salads for yourself.

The fundamental idea is to place the dressing at the bottom of the jar followed by individual ingredients, starting from harder to more delicate food items. The hearty vegetables act as a barrier to prevent the dressing from mixing with the more delicate leaves and benefit from soaking in extra flavor from the dressing. Here is a breakdown of how you should be layering your salad:

1. **Base layer:** Salad dressing. Between one and four tablespoons of your favorite dressing goes in the bottom of the jar

2. **Hardy vegetables and fruits:** Place root vegetables such as carrots and potatoes or other robust choices that hold up well in liquid, such as cucumber and bell pepper, in the next layer.

3. **Beans, grains and pasta:** Fairly firm vegetables like sugar snap peas and chickpeas would be ideal for this layer as they can take the extra weight from the ingredients above. Cooked carbohydrates and grains such as rice and barley could also be placed here as well.

4. **Protein:** Add your cheese, chicken, tofu, or desired protein. If preparing for make-ahead meals, add this layer on the day you intend to consume it.

5. **Salad greens and fruits:** Think baby spinach, parsley, romaine lettuce, sliced strawberries, and blueberries. Feel free tear the greens up and squeeze as much can into the jar. Keeping it compact will help prevent the contents of the jar from sloshing around too much. If preparing for make-ahead meals, add this layer on the day you intend to consume it.

If the layers are carefully arranged, salads can last between three and five days in your fridge without compromising their freshness and quality, although it also depends on the ingredients used. Wetter ingredients such as halved cherry tomatoes and cucumber slices tend to turn slimy more easily, so it is best to consume them as soon as possible. This is also the case for softer cheeses such as feta and fresh mozzarella.

A nifty trick for those who are uncomfortable with transporting the dressing below with the salad can make use of the jar's sealing function by making a parchment cup dressing container. Take a piece of parchment paper and cut it into a square that is slightly bigger than the size of the mouth of the canning jar. Place the parchment paper square on top of the mouth of the jar and gently push it down to create a well to hold the dressing. Secure the paper with an elastic band and then screw the lid on.

When transporting the salads, it is important to keep the jar upright so the dressing and other ingredients can be kept apart. To serve the salad, always give the jar a good shake so the dressing can completely coat all the ingredients. Open the lid and dig in, or if you prefer, you can tip it into a bowl or onto a plate to eat.

Types of Jars to Use

Any canning jar can be used to make jar meals, but there is a dizzying array of jars available in the market that comes in various shapes and sizes. To decide on which jar to use to pack your salads, it will primarily depend on your portion sizes. A basic rule of thumb would be:

- Half pint (4 ounce or 1 cup) jar – breakfast-sized portions
- Pint (16 ounce or 2 cups) jar - Side salads
- Quart (32 ounce or 4 cups) jar - Individual meal portion
- Two quart or larger jars – Multiple/party-size servings

There are also wide- and narrow-mouth jars. The former will be more convenient to not only pack your ingredients into it but also to eat the salad out of the jar.

To seal the jar, there are two types of lids available. The metal ones are the traditional ones that come with a mouth lid and a band to ensure that it is tight fitting. There are also plastic storage caps that could also be used for everyday purposes. They fit right on top of most canning jars and are dishwasher and freezer safe. The latter can be a more convenient solution than metal lids, for they avoid the risk of losing either the band or the metal lid. However, the plastic caps are not vacuum-fit and might not be suitable for canning purposes.

Recipes
Chicken and Spinach Salad

Servings: 2

Ingredients
8 ounces cooked chicken breast, chopped into chunks
2 cups grapes, halved
1/3 cup walnuts, roughly chopped
1/3 cup shaved Parmesan
4 cups baby spinach

Dressing
2 ½ teaspoons red wine vinegar
2 ½ teaspoons country Dijon mustard
½ teaspoon chopped fresh thyme leaves
Salt and pepper, to taste
2 ½ tablespoons extra virgin olive oil

Preparation
1. To make the dressing: Whisk together the vinegar, mustard, thyme, salt and pepper into a small bowl. Slowly drizzle the olive oil into the mixture while constantly stirring until the mixture emulsifies.
2. Divide the dressing equally between 2 quart-sized canning jars. Place the chicken chunks at the bottom of the container, and layer in the grapes, walnuts, cheese, and roughly torn spinach leaves
3. Cover with the lids and you are ready to eat on the go!

Nutritional Facts (315 g per single serving)
Calories 461
Fats 27 g
Carbs 22 g
Protein 47 g
Sodium 461 mg

Buffalo Chicken Salad

Servings: 4

Ingredients

8 teaspoons hot sauce
4 large carrots, diced into bite-size pieces
4 large celery stalks, diced into bite-size pieces
1 red onion, chopped
¾ quart cherry tomatoes, halved
4 cups shredded chicken
4 cups romaine lettuce, chopped

Dressing
¼ cup plain low fat yogurt
1 ounce crumbled blue cheese
2 tablespoons lemon juice
1 clove garlic, minced
½ tablespoon horseradish
Salt and pepper, to taste

Preparation

1. To make the dressing: Whisk together the yogurt, cheese, lemon juice, minced garlic, and horseradish together
2. Divide the dressing among 4 quart-sized canning jars. Add 2 teaspoons of hot sauce to each jar on top of the yogurt dressing
3. Layer the rest of the ingredients in the following order: carrots, celery, onion, cherry tomatoes, chicken, and lettuce.
4. When you are ready to serve, give the jar a good shake to ensure that the salad is thoroughly covered with the dressing.

Nutritional Facts (517 g per single serving)
Calories 352
Fats 8 g
Carbs 19 g
Protein 50 g
Sodium 551 mg

Bacon and Egg Avocado Salad

Servings: 2

Ingredients

½ avocado, diced

1 teaspoon lemon juice

½ cup cherry tomatoes, halved

2 tablespoons flat-leaf parsley, chopped

1 tablespoon chives, chopped

1 hardboiled egg, roughly chopped

1 cup cooked chicken breast, chopped

2 cups romaine, roughly chopped

¼ cup blue cheese, crumbled

2 slices cooked bacon, chopped

Dressing

2 tablespoons lemon juice

½ tablespoon shallot, minced

¼ teaspoon Dijon mustard

Salt and pepper, to taste

3 tablespoons olive oil

Preparation

1. To make the dressing: Whisk the lemon juice, shallot, mustard, salt, and pepper together in a small bowl. Slowly drizzle in the olive oil while constantly stirring until mixture emulsifies.
2. Toss the avocado with lemon juice, to help prevent oxidization.
3. Spoon 3 tablespoons of the dressing into each quart-size canning jar. Layer the tomatoes, parsley, chives, egg, chicken, romaine lettuce, and avocado.

4. Top the salad off with the crumbled blue cheese and bacon.
5. Cover with lid and refrigerate until ready to serve.

Nutritional Facts (629 g per single serving)
Calories 605
Fats 42 g
Carbs 10 g
Protein 38 g
Sodium 678 mg

Spinach with Strawberries and Bacon Salad

Servings: 1

Ingredients
¼ cup red onion, chopped
½ cup strawberries, stems removed, roughly chopped
½ cup cooked bacon, chopped
1 tablespoon pecans, roughly chopped
¼ cup feta cheese
2 cups baby spinach

Dressing
½ tablespoon honey
3 tablespoons olive oil
1 tablespoon balsamic vinegar
Pinch of paprika

Preparation
1. To make the dressing: Whisk together all the dressing ingredients in a small bowl until well combined. Spoon 3 tablespoons of the dressing into a quart-sized canning jar.
2. Put the red onions and strawberries in on the dressing. Next, layer the bacon, pecans, cheese and lastly, top it off with spinach.
3. Cover with the lid and refrigerate.

Nutritional Facts (346 g per single serving)
Calories 840
Fats 72 g
Carbs 29 g
Protein 26 g
Sodium 1240 mg

Creamy Broccoli and Ham Salad

Servings: 2

Ingredients
2 cups broccoli florets
½ cup carrots, sliced
½ cup cucumber, diced
1 cup cherry tomatoes, halved
½ cup edamame
1 cup deli turkey ham, roughly torn
2 cups baby spinach
¼ cup pine nuts

Dressing
1 tablespoon extra-virgin olive oil
2 tablespoons apple cider vinegar
½ tablespoon honey
¼ cup plain Greek yogurt
Salt and pepper, to taste

Preparation
1. In a medium saucepan, some bring water to boil. Add the broccoli florets and cook for 3 minutes, or until crisp-tender. Drain the water and rinse the broccoli under cold water to stop the cooking process. Set it aside to drain.
2. To prepare the dressing: Whisk the dressing ingredients together until well combined. Divide the ingredients evenly between 2 quart-sizes jars.
3. Layer the ingredients in the following order: broccoli, carrots, cucumber, tomatoes, edamame, ham, spinach and pine nuts.
4. To serve, give it a good shake before digging in.

Nutritional Facts (449 g per single serving)
Calories 484
Fats 26 g
Carbs 22 g
Protein 46 g
Sodium 194 mg

Roast Beef and Potato Salad

Servings: 4

Ingredients

7 ounces baby potatoes
1 tablespoon olive oil
8 roast beef slices
8 ounces cherry tomatoes, halved
2 cups salad leaves

Dressing
1 tablespoon horseradish
1 tablespoon red wine vinegar
1 teaspoon Dijon mustard
4 tablespoons olive oil

Preparation
1. Preheat the oven to 350°F
2. Put the baby potatoes on a baking sheet and generously drizzle olive oil to coat them. Place the sheet into the oven and cook for 25 mins, or until they are golden brown and tender in the center. Remove from the oven and let them cool completely.
3. To make the dressing: Whisk together all the dressing ingredients until thoroughly mixed.
4. Divide the dressing among 4 pint-sized jars, followed by a layer of potatoes.
5. Next, add the roast beef, tomatoes, and salad leaves.
6. Cover with the lids, and refrigerate.

Nutritional Facts (303 g per single serving)

Calories 461
Fats 37 g
Carbs 22 g
Protein 14 g
Sodium 532 mg

Thai Beef Noodle Salad Jar

Servings: 4

Ingredients

1 cup broccoli, chopped into small florets
1 ½ cups cooked vermicelli rice noodles
½ pound cooked beef, cut into small cubes
4 scallions, chopped
2 carrots, sliced into matchstick strips
1 yellow bell pepper, chopped
8 baby plum tomatoes, chopped
A handful of fresh cilantro, roughly torn
2 cups mixed spinach and watercress leaves

Dressing
3 tablespoons olive oil
1 tablespoon rice wine vinegar
1 tablespoon peanut butter
1 tablespoon sriracha
2 tablespoons soy sauce
¼ teaspoon ground ginger
1 garlic clove, grated
2 tablespoons honey
1 lime, juice

Preparation

1. To make the dressing: Whisk all the dressing ingredients together until well combined. Divide the mixture evenly into 4 quart-sized canning jars.
2. Layer the rest of the ingredients in the following order: Broccoli, noodles, beef, scallions, carrot, bell pepper, tomatoes, cilantro, and salad leaves.

3. Cover with lids and refrigerate until ready to serve.

Nutritional Facts (402 g per single serving)
Calories 506
Fats 17 g
Carbs 66 g
Protein 22 g
Sodium 782 mg

Minty Turkey and Chickpea Salad

Servings: 2

Ingredients
1 apple, diced and tossed with lemon juice
¼ cup celery, diced
½ cup cucumber, diced
4 tablespoon red onion, finely diced
2 cups cooked turkey, chopped
1 cup garbanzo beans
½ cup chopped tomatoes
4 tablespoons dried cranberries
4 tablespoons chives, chopped

Dressing
1 cup frozen peas
4 tablespoons water
4 large mint leaves, chopped
1 lemon, juice
Salt and pepper, to taste

Preparation
1. Allow the peas to defrost at room temperature for 15 minutes.
2. In a food processor, blend the peas, water, mint, and lemon juice until smooth. Season the dressing with salt and pepper to taste.
3. Divide the dressing between 2 quart-sized mason jars.

4. Layer the rest of the ingredients in the following order: apple, celery, cucumber, onion, turkey, beans, tomatoes, cranberries, and chives.
5. Cover with lids, and refrigerate until ready to serve.

Nutritional Facts (597 g per single serving)
Calories 618
Fats 8 g
Carbs 65 g
Protein 77 g
Sodium 554 mg

Ground Turkey Taco Salad

Servings: 6

Ingredients

½ pound ground turkey
1 tablespoon olive oil
1 teaspoon chili powder
½ teaspoon cumin
¼ teaspoon garlic powder
¼ teaspoon salt
½ cup salsa
2 tablespoons ripe, mashed avocado
½ teaspoon lemon juice
1 cup cherry tomatoes, halved
3 cups romaine lettuce, chopped
½ cup whole grain tortilla chips, broken
½ cup reduced-fat cheddar cheese, shredded

Preparation

1. In a medium skillet, heat the olive oil over medium-high heat. Fry the ground turkey, together with chili powder, cumin, garlic powder, and salt until it is completely cooked. Transfer it to a clean bowl and let it cool completely.
2. In a small bowl, mix the mashed avocado with the lemon juice.
3. Spoon the salsa equally into 6 pint-sized canning jars, followed by the mashed avocado.
4. Next, layer the jars with cooled turkey, tomatoes, and lettuce, and top it off with the broken tortilla chips and shredded cheese.

Nutritional Facts (259 g per single serving)
Calories 278
Fats 17 g
Carbs 11 g
Protein 23 g
Sodium 503 mg

Shrimp Feta Cobb Salad with Ranch Dressing

Servings: 1

Ingredients
8 cherry tomatoes
1 tablespoon red onion, chopped
2 tablespoons cucumber, chopped
1 boiled egg, chopped
1 cup of mixed romaine lettuce and baby spinach
6 cooked shrimp
2 tablespoons feta, crumbled
2 slices of cooked bacon, chopped
2 tablespoons avocado, chopped and sprayed with lime or lemon juice

Dressing
2 tablespoons low-fat buttermilk
1 tablespoon low-fat mayonnaise
¼ teaspoon garlic powder
1 teaspoon chives, finely chopped
Salt and pepper, to taste

Preparation
1. To make the ranch dressing: Whisk together all the dressing ingredients in a small bowl until well combined. Season with salt and pepper to taste.
2. Spoon 3 tablespoons of the dressing into a quart-sized canning jar. Layer the rest of the ingredients as follows: tomatoes, avocado, onions, cucumber, egg, salad leaves, shrimps, feta, and bacon.
3. Cover with a lid and refrigerate.

Nutritional Facts (367 g per single serving)

Calories 459
Fats 31 g
Carbs 14 g
Protein 30 g
Sodium 1046 mg

Peppery Egg and Tuna Salad

Servings: 2

Ingredients
6 boiled eggs, chopped
2/3 cup low-fat mayonnaise
½ cup pickles, chopped
1 can (6 ounces) tuna in water, drained
2 cups arugula
½ cup walnut, chopped
Salt and pepper, to taste

Preparation
1. In a medium bowl, mash the boiled eggs together with the mayonnaise. Season with salt and pepper to taste. Divide the egg mixture evenly into 2 quart-sized mason jars.
2. Finish off by layering the pickles, tuna, arugula, and walnuts
3. Cover with the lids and refrigerate.

Nutritional Facts (360 g per single serving)
Calories 601
Fats 39 g
Carbs 27 g
Protein 42 g
Sodium 1044 mg

Italian Antipasto Salad

Servings: 4

Ingredients
1 quart cherry tomatoes, halved
1 can (14 ounces) artichoke hearts, drained and chopped
3 jars (12 ounces) roasted red peppers, drained and chopped
20 slices of deli meat (such as salami, pepperoni, mortadella, turkey ham), roughly torn
5 ounces provolone cheese, diced
3 cups arugula

Dressing
½ cup olive oil
¼ cup red wine vinegar
Salt and pepper, to taste

Preparation
1. To make the dressing: Whisk the oil, red wine vinegar, salt, and pepper in a small bowl. Divide it among 4 quart-sized canning jars.
2. Layer the ingredients in the following order: cherry tomatoes, artichoke hearts, red peppers, meat, cheese and lastly, arugula.

Nutritional Facts (367 g per single serving)
Calories 515
Fats 45 g
Carbs 12 g
Protein 17 g
Sodium 1516 mg

Smoked Salmon and Sugar Snap Pea Salad

Servings: 4

Ingredients
8 radishes, cut into wedges
¾ pound sugar snap peas, halved
½ red onion, thinly sliced
8 ounces smoked salmon, cut into bite-sized pieces
4 boiled eggs, roughly chopped
8 cups arugula
1 cup alfalfa sprouts

Dressing
½ cup milk
1 tablespoon white wine vinegar
4 ounces cream cheese
1 clove garlic
2 tablespoons mayonnaise
1 tablespoon sesame seeds
1 teaspoon poppy seeds
Salt and pepper, to taste

Preparation
1. To make the dressing: In a food processor, blend the milk, vinegar, cream cheese, garlic, and mayonnaise until smooth. Stir in the sesame and poppy seeds. Season with salt and pepper to taste. Transfer it into a clean bowl and set it aside.

2. In a medium saucepan, boil some water on high heat. Remove the pot from the heat before adding the peas. Cover the pot and allow it to sit for 10 mins. Drain the water and allow the peas to cool down.
3. Spoon equal amounts of the dressing into 4 quart-sized canning jars. Layer the ingredients in the following order: radishes, peas, onions, smoked salmon, egg, arugula and sprouts.
4. Cover with lids and refrigerate.
5. Before serving, give the jar a good shake to toss the dressing with the rest of the ingredients.

Nutritional Facts (341 g per single serving)
Calories 280
Fats 15 g
Carbs 14 g
Protein 23 g
Sodium 649 mg

Ginger Miso Salmon Salad

Servings: 2

Ingredients

2 tablespoons white miso paste
1 tablespoon brown sugar
1 teaspoon freshly grated ginger
1 tablespoon low sodium soy sauce
4 ounces salmon fillet
2 carrots, shredded
½ cup edamame
½ cucumber, diced
8 cups romaine, chopped
¼ cup roasted peanuts

Dressing
2 tablespoons rice wine vinegar
1 tablespoon sesame oil

Preparation

1. Preheat the oven to 350°F.
2. Mix the miso paste, sugar, ginger, and soy sauce in a small bowl until well combined.
3. Place the salmon fillet, skin side down, on a baking sheet and drizzle half the miso mixture over the fish. Place the salmon in the oven for 8-10 minutes, or until cooked. Remove from the oven and allow it to cool.
4. Once cooled, use a fork to break the salmon into large flakes.

5. To make the dressing: Incorporate the rice wine vinegar and sesame oil into the remaining miso mixture. Spoon equal amounts of the dressing into 2 quart-sized canning jars.
6. Pile on the rest of the ingredients in the following order: carrots, edamame, cucumber, salmon, romaine lettuce, and peanuts.
7. Cover with the lids and you are ready to go.

Nutritional Facts (465 g per single serving)
Calories 424
Fats 25 g
Carbs 30 g
Protein 37 g
Sodium 439 mg

Zucchini Quinoa Salad with Avocado Lime Dressing

Servings: 1

Ingredients
1 medium zucchini, spiralized
1/3 cup cooked quinoa
2 teaspoons cilantro, roughly torn
2 scallion stalks, diced
3 asparagus stalks, roughly chopped
¼ cup green peas
¼ cup feta, cubed

Dressing
½ avocado
2 tablespoons almond milk
½ lime, juiced
Salt and pepper, to taste

Preparation
1. To make the dressing: In a food processor, blend all the dressing ingredients until smooth. Season with salt and pepper to taste.
2. In a medium saucepan, bring half a pot of water to a boil. Cook the asparagus and peas for 3-4 minutes. Drain the water and allow the vegetables to cool.
3. To assemble, pour the dressing into a quart-sized mason jar.

4. Add the zucchini to the dressing before layering the quinoa, cilantro, scallion, asparagus, peas, and feta cubes.
5. Cover with a lid and refrigerate until ready to serve.

Nutritional Facts (544g per single serving)
Calories 421
Fats 25 g
Carbs 39 g
Protein 16 g
Sodium 402 mg

Classic Greek salad

Servings: 1

Ingredients
½ cup cucumber, de-seeded and cut into bite-sized pieces
½ cup feta cheese, crumbled
1/3 cup Kalamata olives
½ cup red onion, thinly sliced
½ cup tomato, chopped
1 cup baby spinach and watercress

Dressing
1 tablespoon red wine vinegar
½ tablespoon lemon juice
½ teaspoon Dijon mustard
½ teaspoon dried oregano
2 tablespoons olive oil
Salt and pepper, to taste

Preparation
1. To make the dressing: In a small bowl, whisk the red wine vinegar, lemon juice, mustard, and oregano together. Slowly drizzle in the olive oil until the mixture is well combined. Season with salt and pepper to taste.
2. Spoon 3 tablespoons of the dressing into a quart-sized jar before adding the cucumber. Next layer in the feta cheese, olives, onions, tomatoes and finish it off with the greens
3. Cover with a lid and store the salad in the fridge.

Nutritional Facts (465 g per single serving)
Calories 619
Fats 54 g
Carbs 27 g
Protein 15 g
Sodium 1982 mg

Prawn, Rice and Mango Salad

Servings: 1

Ingredients
½ cup cooked brown rice
6 cooked prawns
¼ ripe mango, cut into bite-sized chunks
½ red chili, deseeded and finely chopped
1 cup baby spinach
Handful of cilantro, roughly chopped

Dressing
½ tablespoon low-salt soy sauce
1 teaspoon sesame oil
1 teaspoon rice vinegar
½ teaspoon honey

Preparation
1. To make the dressing: Whisk together all the dressing ingredients until well combined. Spoon the mixture into a quart-sized canning jar.
2. Place the rice in the bottom of the jar, before layering with the prawns, mango, chili, spinach and cilantro, in that order.
3. Cover with a lid and refrigerate.

Nutritional Facts (341 g per single serving)
Calories 291
Fats 6 g
Carbs 50 g
Protein 16 g
Sodium 328 mg

Refreshing Caprese Salad in a Jar

Servings: 4

Ingredients
4 cups cherry tomatoes
8 ounces fresh mozzarella, roughly torn
8 cups baby spinach
2 cups fresh basil

Dressing
¼ cup balsamic vinegar
¾ cup olive oil
Salt and pepper, to taste

Preparation
1. To make the dressing: Pour all the ingredients together in a quart-sized mason jar, and give it a vigorous shake. Taste and adjust the seasoning if necessary. Divide the dressing evenly among three other quart-sized jars.
2. Add the cherry tomatoes, mozzarella, spinach, and basil, in that order.
3. Cover with lids and store in the fridge until ready to serve.

Nutritional Facts (344 g per single serving)
Calories 584
Fats 53 g
Carbs 14 g
Protein 16 g
Sodium 415 mg

Black Bean and Corn Salad

Servings: 4

Ingredients
2 avocados, cut into bite-sized pieces
2 teaspoons lemon juice
4 cups cherry tomatoes, halved
1 red onion, diced
2 cans (16 ounces) black beans, drained and rinsed
8 ounces corn
4 ounces pepper jack cheese, cut into bite-sized pieces
4 cups romaine lettuce, chopped
¼ cup cilantro, chopped

Dressing
8 ounces salsa
8 tablespoons plain Greek yogurt

Preparation
1. Toss the avocado with the lemon juice, and set it aside.
2. In each of 4 quart-sized jars, mix 2 ounces of salsa with 2 tablespoons of yogurt for the dressing.
3. Next, layer the tomatoes, onions, black beans, corn, avocado, cheese, romaine and cilantro, in that order.
4. Store the jars in the refrigerator until you're ready to eat.

Nutritional Facts (679 g per single serving)
Calories 506
Fats 20 g
Carbs 61 g
Protein 26 g
Sodium 905 mg

Sweet Potato Salad

Servings: 1

Ingredients
1 sweet potato, cut into bite-sized pieces
1 tablespoon olive oil
Salt and pepper, to taste
1 tablespoon scallions, sliced
1 teaspoon minced fresh mint leaves
½ fresh jalapeno to taste
2 tablespoons raisins
1 cup baby spinach

Dressing
½ red bell pepper, deseeded and roughly chopped
1 ½ tablespoons red wine vinegar
1 tablespoon olive oil
1 teaspoons ground cumin
½ tablespoon orange zest

Preparation
1. Preheat the oven to 375°F.
2. Place the sweet potato pieces on a baking sheet and toss them with olive oil, salt, and pepper. Roast for 30 minutes, or until cooked. Remove from the oven and let them cool a little.
3. To make the dressing: In a food processor, blend the red bell pepper with red wine vinegar, olive oil, cumin, and orange zest.
4. While the sweet potatoes are still warm, toss them with the dressing
5. Place the sweet potatoes in a pint-sized jar and allow it to cool completely.

6. Add the scallions, mint, jalapeno, raisins, and spinach.
7. Secure the jar with the lid and store it in the fridge.

Nutritional Facts (315 g per single serving)
Calories 459
Fats 27 g
Carbs 52 g
Protein 5 g
Sodium 104 mg

Chickpea Salad with Mint Yogurt Dressing

Servings: 4

Ingredients
2 cups chickpeas, drained and rinsed
½ cup red onion, thinly sliced
1 green bell pepper, chopped
1 cup cucumber, chopped
⅓ cup crumbled feta cheese
4 cups baby spinach
½ cup flat-leaf parsley, chopped

Dressing
½ cup plain Greek yogurt
1 tablespoon lemon juice
1 clove garlic, coarsely chopped
¼ cup mint leaves
Salt and pepper, to taste

Preparation
1. To make the dressing: In a food processor, whizz all the dressing ingredients up until smooth. Season with salt and pepper to taste. Divide the dressing equally among 4 pint-sized jars.
2. Layer the rest of the ingredients in the following order: chickpeas, onion, bell pepper, cucumber, cheese, spinach, and parsley.
3. Cover the jars with lids and store them in the fridge.

Nutritional Facts (232 g per single serving)
Calories 193
Fats 5 g
Carbs 18 g
Protein 13 g
Sodium 356 mg

Crunchy Green Bean and Feta Salad

Servings: 1

Ingredients

2 cups green beans
¾ cup cherry tomatoes, halved
¼ cup shallots, thinly sliced
2 ounces crumbled feta cheese
6 basil leaves, sliced

Dressing
1 tablespoon balsamic vinegar
1 teaspoon honey
3 tablespoons olive oil
Salt and pepper, to taste

Preparation

1. Over high heat, bring a pot of water to boil. Meanwhile, trim the green beans top and tail, and then cut them in half.
2. Drop the beans into the boiling water and cook for 5 mins. Drain the water and run the beans under cold water to stop further cooking. Set the beans aside and allow them to cool completely.
3. To make dressing: In a small bowl, combine the balsamic vinegar and honey. Slowly drizzle in the olive oil while whisking continuously, until the mixture emulsifies. Season with salt and pepper to taste. Spoon 3 tablespoons of the dressing into a quart-sized jar.

4. Next, add the cherry tomatoes, shallots, green beans, cheese and top it off with basil.
5. To serve, shake the jar vigorously so the salad ingredients are coated with the dressing.

Nutritional Facts (625 g per single serving)
Calories 647
Fats 41 g
Carbs 57 g
Protein 38 g
Sodium 599 mg

Rainbow Avocado Salad with Citrus Dressing

Servings: 4

Ingredients
1 avocado, diced and sprayed with lime or lemon juice
1 teaspoon lemon juice
2 cucumbers, diced
1 cup red cabbage, shredded
1 cup cooked edamame
8 yellow mini bell peppers, core removed and sliced in rings
1 cup cooked artichoke hearts, roughly chopped
1 1/3 cup cherry tomatoes, halved

Dressing
3 tablespoons fresh lime juice
1 tablespoon Dijon mustard
1 clove garlic, minced
2 tablespoons olive oil
8 basil leaves, minced
Salt and pepper, to taste

Preparation
1. Combine the avocado with the lemon juice and toss to coat, to help prevent discoloration.
2. To make the dressing: In a small bowl, combine the lime juice, mustard, garlic, and basil leaves. Slowly drizzle in the olive oil while whisking the mixture constantly until well blended.
3. Spoon 2 tablespoons of dressing into each of the 4 pint-sized jars.

4. Layer the rest of the salad ingredients in the following order: cucumbers, cabbage, edamame, peppers, artichoke, tomatoes, and avocado.
5. Cover with lids, and refrigerate them until ready to serve.

Nutritional Facts (380 g per single serving)
Calories 263
Fats 16 g
Carbs 22 g
Protein 7 g
Sodium 98 mg

Tofu and Bell Pepper Salad

Servings: 2

Ingredients
½ cup extra firm tofu
½ cup bell pepper, halved
½ cucumber, chopped
½ cup lentil sprouts
1 cup romaine lettuce, chopped
1 tablespoon fresh parsley, chopped
¼ cup pumpkin seeds

Dressing
1 tablespoon tahini
1 tablespoon lemon juice
Pinch of red pepper flakes
1 teaspoon olive oil
1 teaspoon honey
¼ teaspoon oregano
1 garlic clove, minced
Salt and pepper, to taste

Preparation
1. To make the dressing: In a small bowl, whisk together all the dressing ingredients. Spoon 2 tablespoons of dressing into each of 2 pint-sized jars.
2. Add the tofu, bell pepper, cucumber, sprouts, lettuce, parsley, and pumpkin seeds, in order.
3. Cover and refrigerate them until ready to serve.

Nutritional Facts (253 g per single serving)
Calories 247
Fats 15 g
Carbs 17 g
Protein 21 g
Sodium 22 mg

Red Pesto Zucchini Noodle Salad

Servings: 2

Ingredients

1 cup artichoke hearts, drained and quartered
¼ red onion, sliced thinly
¾ cup chickpeas, drained and rinsed
2 cups baby spinach
¼ cup Kalamata olives, pitted and halved
¼ cup crumbled feta cheese
1 large zucchini, spiralized

Dressing
½ cup sundried tomatoes
1 tablespoon pine nuts
¼ cup extra-virgin olive oil
Salt and pepper, to taste

Preparation

1. To make the dressing: In a food processor, blend all the dressing ingredients into a smooth paste. Taste and adjust the seasonings based on your preference.
2. Spoon 4 tablespoons of dressing each into 2 half-gallon sized canning jars.
3. Add the artichoke hearts, onion, chickpeas, spinach, olives, cheese, and zucchini noodles in order
4. Cover with lids and refrigerate them. To serve, toss everything together before eating.

Nutritional Facts (390 g per single serving)
Calories 557
Fats 41 g
Carbs 40 g
Protein 15 g
Sodium 958 mg

Pomegranate and Pear Feta Salad

Servings: 1

Ingredients
½ cup pomegranate seeds
1 pear, cored and thinly sliced
3 cups spinach leaves
¼ cup pecans, roughly chopped
½ cup crumbled blue cheese

Dressing
1 tablespoon red wine vinegar
3 tablespoons olive oil
Salt and pepper, to taste

Preparation
1. To make the dressing: Whisk the red wine vinegar, while slowly drizzling in the olive oil until the mixture emulsifies. Season with salt and pepper to taste.
2. Spoon 3 tablespoons of dressing into a quart-sized canning jar.
3. Add the pomegranate seeds, pear slices, spinach leaves, blue cheese, and pecans
4. Cover and refrigerate until ready to serve.

Nutritional Facts (463g per single serving)
Calories 861
Fats 73 g
Carbs 51 g
Protein 15 g
Sodium 464 mg

Rainbow Fruit Salad

Servings: 1

Ingredients
1 orange
½ cup fresh mango, cut into bite-size piece
½ cup grapes, halved
1 kiwi fruit, peeled and sliced
½ cup blueberries
¼ cup strawberries, sliced
½ cup raspberries

Preparation
1. Into a quart-sized jar, squeeze the juice of half an orange. Peel and dice the other half into bite-sized pieces and throw them into the jar.
2. Place the mango cubes on top of the oranges, followed by the grapes, kiwi, blueberries, strawberries, and raspberries. Try to pack it as full as possible to prevent the fruits from oxidizing.
3. Cover with a lid and refrigerate it.

Nutritional Facts (475 g per single serving)
Calories 423
Fats 18 g
Carbs 60 g
Protein 5 g
Sodium 8 mg

Camembert Grape Salad with Honey Vinaigrette

Servings: 4

Ingredients
¾ pound seedless grapes, halved
¾ pound fresh figs, sliced
4 ounces camembert, cut into cubes
½ cup pecan, roughly chopped
2 quarts arugula

Dressing
¼ cup honey
¼ cup red wine vinegar
½ cup olive oil
2 tablespoons orange juice
1 tablespoon poppy seeds

Preparation
1. To make the dressing, whisk together all the ingredients until well combined. Divide the dressing evenly among 4 quart-sized jars.
2. Layer the rest of the salad ingredients in the following order: grapes, figs, cheese, arugula, and pecans.
3. Seal and refrigerate until ready to serve.

Nutritional Facts (322 g per single serving)
Calories 562
Fats 45 g
Carbs 37 g
Protein 10 g
Sodium 256 mg

Spinach, Blueberry and Blue Cheese Salad

Servings: 1

Ingredients
½ cup blueberries
3 cups spinach leaves
½ cup crumbled blue cheese
¼ cup sliced almonds

Dressing
2 tablespoons red wine vinegar
½ tablespoon shallot, minced
3 tablespoons olive oil
Salt and pepper, to taste

Preparation
1. To make the dressing: Whisk together the red wine vinegar and shallot in a small bowl, while slowly drizzling in the olive oil until the dressing emulsifies. Season with salt and pepper, to taste.
2. Spoon 3 tablespoons of the dressing into a quart-sized jar.
3. Add the blueberries into the container, followed by the spinach, blue cheese, and almonds.
4. Refrigerate the salad until ready to consume.

Nutritional Facts (268 g per single serving)
Calories 553
Fats 44 g
Carbs 20 g
Protein 23 g
Sodium 846 mg

Strawberry Goat Cheese Salad

Servings: 1

Ingredients
2/3 cup strawberries, sliced
3 cups spinach
1/3 cup walnuts, roughly chopped
½ cup goat cheese, crumbled

Dressing

1 tablespoon balsamic vinegar
½ tablespoon honey
3 tablespoons olive oil
Salt and pepper, to taste

Preparation
1. To make a parchment paper cup for the dressing: Place a quart-sized canning jar on top of a piece of parchment paper. Trace a square around the jar, making sure that it is slightly bigger than the mouth of the jar. Cut the square parchment paper out.
2. To make the dressing: Mix the balsamic vinegar with honey in a small bowl. Drizzle in the olive oil while whisking continuously until the dressing thickens. Season with salt and pepper, to taste.
3. Layer the strawberry slices in the bottom of a quart-sized jar. Next, add half the spinach, followed by the walnuts, the remaining spinach, and then the goat cheese.

4. Take the prepared parchment paper and press it down into the mouth of the canning jar as much as possible, with the edges still around the outside of the jar. Secure the paper with an elastic band.
5. Spoon 3 tablespoons of the dressing into the parchment paper cup. Cover securely with a lid and refrigerate the salad.

Nutritional Facts (370 g per single serving)
Calories 846
Fats 73 g
Carbs 16 g
Protein 38 g
Sodium 544 mg

Lemon Pesto Pasta Salad in a Jar

Servings: 2

Ingredients
¼ cup diced tomatoes
¼ cup Kalamata olives, pitted and sliced
½ cup cooked chicken breast, roughly diced
2 cups cooked pasta
¼ cup grated Parmesan cheese
2 cups spinach

Pesto
½ cup spinach
¼ cup olive oil
6 tablespoons cashews, chopped
¼ cup grated Parmesan cheese
1 garlic clove
½ lemon, juice
Salt and pepper, to taste

Preparation
1. To make the pesto: In a food processor, combine the spinach, olive oil, cashews, cheese, and garlic. Pulse until smooth. Squeeze in the juice of half a lemon, and season with salt and pepper to taste. Pulse one more time until all the ingredients are well incorporated.
2. Divide the pesto evenly between 2 quart-sized canning jars.

3. Place the tomatoes on top of the pesto, then put in the olives, chicken, and pasta. Top it off with spinach.
4. Refrigerate the salad. Before serving, give the jar a good shake to toss the pasta with the pesto.

Nutritional Facts (340 g per single serving)
Calories 911
Fats 63 g
Carbs 56 g
Protein 35 g
Sodium 999 mg

Chicken and Orzo Salad with Creamy Citrus Dressing

Servings: 2

Ingredients
2 roasted red peppers, diced
1 cup red onion, finely chopped
2 cups cooked orzo
1 chicken breast, shredded
2 cups fresh spinach

Dressing
2 tablespoons Greek yogurt
¼ cup orange juice
1 ½ teaspoon orange zest
1 teaspoon balsamic vinegar
2 tablespoons olive oil
Salt and pepper, to taste

Preparation
1. To make the dressing: In a small bowl, whisk together all the dressing ingredients until thoroughly mixed.
2. Spoon 3 tablespoons of the dressing into each of 2 quart-sized canning jars.
3. Layer the rest of the ingredients in the following order: red peppers, onions, pasta, chicken, and spinach.
4. Refrigerate the salad, and when ready to serve, give it a thorough shake to mix the dressing with the pasta salad.

Nutritional Facts (444 g per single serving)
Calories 527
Fats 18 g
Carbs 54 g
Protein 37 g
Sodium 103 mg

Spinach, Snap Peas, and Orzo Salad

Servings: 4

Ingredients
1 cup orzo
2 ½ cups cherry tomatoes, halved
1 cup snap peas, halved
8 ounces fresh mozzarella balls
5 ounces baby spinach, roughly torn

Dressing
3 tablespoons olive oil
2 teaspoons grated lemon zest
1 tablespoon lemon juice
½ cup flat-leaf parsley, chopped
Salt and pepper, to taste

Preparation
1. In a medium saucepan, bring a pot of salted water to a boil and cook the orzo according to the packaging directions. Drain off the excess water and set it aside in a clean bowl.
2. To make the dressing: In a small bowl, whisk together all the dressing ingredients until well combined. Spoon 3 tablespoons of the dressing into each of 4 quart-sized canning jars.
3. Layer the cherry tomatoes on top of the dressing, followed by the cooked pasta, snap peas, mozzarella, and spinach.
4. Screw the lid on and refrigerate the salad.

Nutritional Facts (406 g per single serving)
Calories 386
Fats 12 g
Carbs 45 g
Protein 27 g
Sodium 459 mg

Sundried Tomato Pesto and Salami Pasta Salad

Servings: 1

Ingredients

¾ cup pasta
1 tablespoon sundried tomato pesto
1 teaspoon olive oil
¾ cup cherry tomatoes, halved
4 black olives, halved
4 slices salami, sliced
½ cup fresh mozzarella, roughly torn
Hand of basil leaves
1 cup spinach

Preparation

1. Bring a medium pot of salted water to a boil and cook the pasta according to the packaging directions. Drain off the excess water and set it aside in a clean bowl.
2. Toss the pasta with the pesto and olive oil, making sure that it is thoroughly combined.
3. Transfer the prepared pesto to the bottom of a quart-sized jar. Layer the rest of the ingredients in this order: cherry tomatoes, olives, salami, mozzarella, basil, and spinach.
4. Refrigerate the salad, and it is ready to be eaten anytime.

Nutritional Facts (484 g per single serving)
Calories 750
Fats 38 g
Carbs 60 g
Protein 43 g
Sodium 1974 mg

Creamy Chicken Caesar Pasta Salad

Servings: 1

Ingredients
½ avocado, diced
1 teaspoon lemon juice
1 cup cooked pasta
¾ cup cucumber, diced
¼ cup cherry tomatoes, halved
1 cup cooked chicken breast, cut into chunks
¾ cup romaine lettuce, chopped into bite-sized pieces
1 tablespoon Parmesan cheese

Dressing
1 garlic cloves
3 anchovy fillets (packed in olive oil)
1 lemon, zest and juice
½ large egg yolk
Salt
1 cup extra-virgin olive oil

Preparation
1. In a small bowl, stir the avocado with the lemon juice, and set it aside.
2. To make the dressing: In a food processor, blend the garlic, anchovies and the zest of lemon until it becomes a thick paste. Drop the egg yolk, a pinch of salt and a tablespoon of lemon juice into the paste and blend it on slow speed. While blending, slowly drizzle in a ¼ cup of the olive oil. The mixture should look thick and creamy at this point. Squeeze in another tablespoon of lemon juice, and continue blending on low speed. Drizzle in

another ¼ cup of the oil before adding more lemon juice.
3. Repeat the process until all the oil is incorporated. The dressing should now take on the consistency of heavy cream. Taste, and season with salt and lemon juice if needed.
4. Spoon two tablespoons of the dressing into a quart-sized jar, and refrigerate the rest. Add the pasta, cucumber, cherry tomatoes, chicken, avocado, lettuce, and cheese, in that order.
5. When you are ready to serve, shake the jar thoroughly to combine.

Nutritional Facts (567 g per single serving)
Calories 832
Fats 47 g
Carbs 52 g
Protein 55 g
Sodium 263 mg

Spinach and Fresh Mozzarella Pasta Salad

Servings: 4

Ingredients

4 cups cherry tomatoes, halved
8 ounces fresh mozzarella, roughly torn
2 cups dry whole wheat pasta
8 cups baby spinach

Dressing
2 tablespoons honey
1/3 cup balsamic vinegar
1 cup olive oil

Preparation

1. In a medium saucepan, boil some salted water. Cook the pasta as per the packaging instructions. Drain the water and set the pasta aside to cool down.
2. To make the dressing: In a medium bowl, incorporate the honey with the balsamic vinegar. Drizzle the olive oil slowly into the mixture while constantly whisking it, until the dressing thickens.
3. Spoon 2 tablespoons of the dressing into each of the 4 quart-sized jars.
4. Layer the rest of the ingredients in this order: cherry tomatoes, mozzarella, pasta, and spinach.
5. Cover with lids and refrigerate.

Nutritional Facts (420 g per single serving)
Calories 754
Fats 56 g
Carbs 52 g
Protein 18 g
Sodium 275 mg

Pearl Couscous and Roasted Beetroot Salad

Servings: 4

Ingredients
4 raw beets
1 1/3 cup pearl couscous
½ small red onion, thinly sliced
2 tablespoons feta
¼ cup fresh flat-leaf parsley, chopped
2 tablespoons sliced almonds, toasted

Dressing
2 tablespoons pomegranate molasses
1 tablespoon lemon juice
5 tablespoons olive oil
1 teaspoon honey

Preparation
1. Preheat the oven to 350°F.
2. Slice the leaves off the beets and give them a good scrub. Wrap the beets loosely with aluminum foil.
3. Transfer the beets to a baking sheet and roast them for 50-60 mins. During roasting, check the beets every 20 minutes to make sure they do not dry out. If necessary, drizzle a tablespoon of water over them before wrapping once again to continue cooking. Insert a fork or skewer into the beet to test for its doneness. The fork or skewer should slide easily through the beet if it is cooked.

4. Once cooked, set the beets aside and let them cool completely before handling them. To peel the skin, place a beet in a paper towel and rub the skin away. It should peel away easily; otherwise, roast it a little longer. Cut the beets into wedges.
5. While the beets are roasting, cook the pearl couscous. In a medium saucepan, bring a pot of water to a boil. Lower the heat to medium-high before adding the pearl couscous. Cook it for 15 minutes. Drain the water and transfer it to a clean plate to cool.
6. To make the dressing: In a medium bowl, whisk all the dressing ingredients together until well incorporated. Spoon 3 tablespoons of the dressing into each of 4 pint-sized jars.
7. Layer the beets on top of the dressing, then add the onions, feta, couscous, parsley, and almonds, in that order.
8. Cover with lids, and refrigerate.

Nutritional Facts (286 g per single serving)
Calories 325
Fats 3 g
Carbs 67 g
Protein 9 g
Sodium 157 mg

Italian Tortellini Salad

Servings: 4

Ingredients
4 cups cherry tomatoes, halved
1 red onion, chopped
1 cup green olives, sliced
4 ounces cheese tortellini
1 cup salami, sliced
4 ounces goat cheese
4 cups arugula

Dressing
1 teaspoon honey
¾ cup olive oil
¼ cup red wine vinegar
2 tablespoons Parmesan cheese, grated
1 tablespoon dried parsley

Preparation
1. Bring a medium-sized pot of salted water to a boil. Cook the tortellini as per the package instructions. Drain the water, and rinse the pasta under cold water to stop it from overcooking. Set the tortellini aside in a clean bowl.
2. To make the dressing: In a medium bowl, whisk together all the dressing ingredients until the olive oil is well incorporated. Spoon 3 tablespoons of the dressing into each of 4 quart-sized canning jars.

3. Place the tomatoes on top of the dressing, followed by the onions, olives, tortellini, salami, goat cheese, and arugula.
4. Cover with lids, and refrigerate.

Nutritional Facts (400 g per single serving)
Calories 758
Fats 65 g
Carbs 28 g
Protein 17 g
Sodium 1382 mg

Kale and Arugula Citrus Couscous Salad

Servings: 2

Ingredients
2 celery stalks, diced
1 cup roasted cauliflower, cut into florets
2 oranges, cut into bite-sized pieces
2 cups whole wheat couscous, cooked
1 cup feta cheese, crumbled
2 cups baby kale
2 cups arugula

Dressing
3 tablespoons olive oil
1 tablespoon balsamic vinegar
1 teaspoon maple syrup
Salt and pepper, to taste

Preparation
1. To make the dressing: In a medium bowl, whisk together all the dressing ingredients until the olive oil is well incorporated. Spoon 2 tablespoons of the dressing in each of 2 quart-sized canning jars.
2. Fill the jar with the rest of the ingredients in the following order: celery, cauliflower, oranges, couscous, feta, kale, and arugula.
3. Seal and refrigerate.

Nutritional Facts (266 g per single serving)
Calories 331
Fats 19 g
Carbs 33 g
Protein 10 g
Sodium 379 mg

Ranch Chicken Pasta Salad

Servings: 2

Ingredients

6 ounces cooked pasta shells
6 ounces cooked chicken, chopped into bite-sized pieces
1 red bell pepper, chopped
2 cups baby spinach

Dressing
½ cup Greek yogurt
½ cup sour cream
1 lemon, juice
2 tablespoons parsley, minced
2 teaspoons fresh chives, minced
½ teaspoon dried dill
½ teaspoon onion powder
½ teaspoon garlic powder
Salt and pepper, to taste

Preparation

1. To make the dressing: In a medium bowl, whisk together all the dressing ingredients until thoroughly mixed. Season with salt and pepper to taste.
2. Toss the cooked pasta with the dressing.
3. Divide the pasta between 2 quart-sized canning jars. Next, add the chicken and bell pepper, and finish it off with the spinach.
4. Cover with lids and refrigerate until ready to eat.

Nutritional Facts (380 g per single serving)
Calories 415
Fats 10 g
Carbs 38 g
Protein 42 g
Sodium 160 mg

Farro and Chickpea salad

Servings: 5

Ingredients
1 ¼ cups farro
1 tablespoon olive oil
1 tablespoon lemon juice
Salt
2 cans (15 ounces) chickpeas, drained and rinsed
4 stalks celery, roughly chopped
1 small red onion, chopped
1 cup flat-leaf parsley, chopped
4 cups of spinach and arugula salad mix
4 tablespoons of Kalamata olives, pitted and thinly sliced
A handful of dried cranberries

Dressing
1 cup extra-virgin olive oil
½ cup red wine vinegar
4 cloves garlic, minced
1 tablespoon dried oregano
2 teaspoons Dijon mustard
1 teaspoon honey
Salt and pepper, to taste

Preparation
1. Soak the farro in cold water for 20 minutes. Drain off the water and toss the faro into a medium saucepan. Add enough fresh water to cover. Bring the water to a boil and allow the farro to simmer for 20 minutes, or until tender. Drain oft the water and transfer the farro to a clean bowl. Season it with olive oil, lemon juice, and salt, to taste.
2. To make the dressing: In a medium bowl, whisk together all the dressing ingredients until completely mixed. Season with salt and pepper to taste.
3. In a medium bowl, toss the chickpeas, celery, red onion, and parsley, with 1/3 cup of the dressing.
4. Spoon 1 tablespoon of the dressing into each of 5 quart-sized jars. Divide the dressed chickpeas among the jars before adding the farro, salad leaves, olives, and cranberries.
5. Cover with lids and refrigerate.

Nutritional Facts (328 g per single serving)
Calories 765
Fats 51 g
Carbs 62 g
Protein 16 g
Sodium 445 mg

Farro, Cabbage and Apple Salad

Servings: 2

Ingredients
1 cup farro
½ tablespoon olive oil
8 ounces shredded red cabbage
2 small green apples, cut into cubes
½ cup dried cranberries
¼ cup shelled pistachios

Dressing
1/3 cup reduced fat mayonnaise
¼ cup milk
3 tablespoons white wine vinegar
3 tablespoons honey
1 tablespoon poppy seeds

Preparation
1. Soak the farro in cold water for 20 minutes. Drain off the water and toss the faro into a medium saucepan. Add enough fresh water to cover the grains. Bring the water to boil and allow the farro to simmer for 20 minutes, or until tender. Drain off the water and transfer it to a clean bowl. Season it with olive oil.
2. To make the dressing: In a small bowl, whisk together all the dressing ingredients until completely mixed. Season with salt and pepper to taste.
3. Spoon 3 tablespoons of the dressing into each of the 2 quart-sized jars.

4. Divide the rest of the ingredients equally and in the following order: farro, cabbage, apples, cranberries, and pistachios.
5. Cover with lids and place in refrigerator until ready to serve.

Nutritional Facts (493 g per single serving)
Calories 990
Fats 33 g
Carbs 159 g
Protein 19 g
Sodium 731 mg

Quinoa-Chia Curry Salad

Servings: 1

Ingredients

Quinoa
1 cup quinoa
1 tablespoon olive oil
1 medium onion, chopped
3 garlic cloves, minced
2 cups water
Salt and pepper, to taste

Salad
½ cup quinoa
1 tablespoon raisins
¼ cup red bell pepper, chopped
¼ cup canned chickpeas, rinsed and drained
1 tablespoon pine nuts, toasted
1 cup romaine lettuce

Dressing
1 teaspoon olive oil
1 teaspoon white wine vinegar
1/8 teaspoon kosher salt
¾ teaspoon curry powder
½ teaspoon chia seeds

Preparation

1. Using a fine-mesh strainer, run the quinoa under cold water until the water comes out clear. Drain off the excess water and set the quinoa aside in a clean bowl.
2. In a medium saucepan, heat 1 tablespoon of olive oil over medium-high heat. Add the onions and cook for about 5 minutes, or until they become translucent, before tossing in the minced garlic to fry for another minute.
3. Add the quinoa, water, salt, and pepper. Bring the water to a boil, then reduce the heat to low, cover with a lid, and allow the quinoa to simmer for 15 minutes. Remove the pot from the heat and allow it to steam for 5 minutes. Using a fork, fluff the cooked quinoa up. Set aside to cool completely.
4. To make the dressing: In a small bowl, whisk together all the dressing ingredients until thoroughly combined. Pour the dressing into a pint-sized canning jar.
5. Add the quinoa, followed by the raisins, bell pepper, chickpeas, pine nuts, and romaine lettuce.
6. Cover with a lid and refrigerate.

Nutritional Facts (278 g per single serving)

Calories 274
Fats 9 g
Carbs 41 g
Protein 6 g
Sodium 115 mg

Quinoa Burrito Bowl Salad

Servings: 5

Ingredients
2 tablespoons coconut oil, divided
2 large chicken breasts
2 teaspoons sea salt
1 sweet potato, peeled and cut into bite-sized chunks
5 tablespoons plain Greek yogurt
3 cups quinoa, cooked
½ cup chopped fresh cilantro
¾ cup shredded mozzarella cheese
3 cups lettuce, chopped

Preparation
1. In a medium skillet, heat 1 tablespoon of coconut oil over high heat. Place the chicken breasts in the pan and season them with the sea salt. Cook for about 4 minutes on each side, until they turn golden brown on the outside and are no longer pink on the inside. Remove from heat and allow them to cool.
2. Once completely cooled, cut the meat up into bite-sized pieces.
3. In the same skillet, melt another tablespoon of coconut oil over medium heat. Brown the sweet potato on all sides, about 3-5 minutes, and then reduce the heat to medium-low heat and cover the pan with a lid. Cook until the potatoes become fork tender, about 5 minutes.
4. To assemble, spoon 1 tablespoon of Greek yogurt into each of the 5 pint-sized jars.

5. Layer the sweet potatoes in, followed by the quinoa, cilantro, mozzarella, chicken and lettuce.
6. Cover with lids and refrigerate.

Nutritional Facts (246 g per single serving)
Calories 352
Fats 10 g
Carbs 30 g
Protein 34 g
Sodium 205 mg

Roasted Sweet Potato with Quinoa Salad

Servings: 1

Ingredients
1 sweet potato, diced into bite-sized pieces
1 tablespoon olive oil
Salt and pepper, to taste
½ cup black beans
1 cup cooked quinoa
¼ red pepper, diced
1 cup baby spinach
1 tablespoon dried cranberries
1 tablespoon sunflower seeds

Dressing
¾ cup mango, fresh or frozen
1 tablespoon balsamic vinegar
1 ½ tablespoons water

Preparation
1. Preheat the oven to 375°F.
2. Place the sweet potato pieces on a baking sheet and toss them with olive oil, salt and pepper. Place the sheet into the oven and roast for 30 minutes, or until the potatoes are cooked. Remove it from the oven and let it cool completely
3. To make the dressing: In a food processor, blend the mango with the balsamic vinegar and water.
4. Pour the black beans into a quart-sized jar, followed by quinoa and roasted sweet potatoes.

5. Pour the dressing in, then the red pepper, spinach, cranberries, and sunflower seeds.
6. Secure the jar with a lid and store it in the fridge.

Nutritional Facts (670 g per single serving)
Calories 757
Fats 23 g
Carbs 123 g
Protein 22 g
Sodium 283 mg

Tabbouleh Quinoa Salad

Servings: 2

Ingredients
2 cups cooked quinoa
1 bunch (1 ¼ cups) flat-leaf parsley, chopped
1 large cucumber, cut into ¼-inch pieces
2 Roma tomatoes, deseeded and chopped
3 scallions

Dressing
¼ cup lemon juice
1 tablespoon garlic, finely minced
Salt and pepper, to taste
¼ cup extra virgin olive oil

Preparation
1. To make the dressing: In a small bowl, mix the lemon juice with garlic, salt, and pepper. Slowly drizzle in the olive oil while whisking the mixture continuously until the dressing thickens.
2. In a large bowl, combine the rest of the salad ingredients and toss them with the dressing. Taste, and adjust the salt and pepper according to your personal preference.
3. Divide the tabbouleh equally between 2 quart-sized jars.
4. Secure the jars with lids and refrigerate.

Nutritional Facts (485 g per single serving)
Calories 515
Fats 32 g
Carbs 52 g
Protein 11 g
Sodium 44 mg

Barley and Kale Salad

Servings: 1

Ingredients

½ cup quick-cooking barley

1 cup water

2 ½ tablespoons red onion, diced

½ cup cucumber slices, quartered

½ cup cherry tomatoes, halved

½ cup red bell pepper, diced

2 cups kale, ribs removed and roughly chopped

Dressing

1 tablespoon white wine vinegar

1 ½ tablespoons olive oil

Salt and pepper, to taste

Preparation

1. In a medium saucepan, bring 1 cup of salted water to boil. Pour the barley into the boiling water and reduce the heat to low. Cover with a lid and allow the barley to continue simmering for 10-15 minutes, or until all the water has evaporated. Remove from the heat, and set it aside to let it cool completely.
2. To make the dressing: In a small bowl, mix the white wine vinegar with salt and pepper. Slowly drizzle in the olive oil while whisking the mixture continuously until the dressing thickens. Spoon 3 tablespoons of the dressing into a quart-sized jar.

3. Layer the rest of the ingredients in the following order: onions, cucumber, cherry tomatoes, barley, red bell pepper, and kale.
4. Cover with a lid and refrigerate until ready to eat.

Nutritional Facts (368 g per single serving)
Calories 574
Fats 24 g
Carbs 82 g
Protein 16 g
Sodium 31 mg

Barley, Feta, and Asparagus Salad

Servings: 4

Ingredients

1 cup uncooked pearl barley
2 ½ cups water
½ teaspoon salt
1 tablespoon cooking oil
12 spears asparagus
4 cups cherry tomatoes, quartered
8 ounces feta cheese, diced
1 cup olives, pitted and chopped
2 tablespoons flat-leaf parsley, finely chopped
4 tablespoons extra virgin olive oil

Preparation

1. In a medium saucepan, bring the 2 ½ cups of water an ½ teaspoon of salt to a boil over high heat. Add the barley into the boiling water and reduce the heat to low. Cover with a lid and allow the barley to continue simmering for 40 mins. Turn the heat off and leave the lid on for 5 minutes. Remove the lid, give it a stir, and drain off any excess liquid (if necessary). Set it aside to let it cool completely.
2. In a medium saucepan, heat the cooking oil over medium heat and fry the asparagus until tender.
3. To assemble, divide the asparagus evenly between 4 quart-sized jars. Next, add the barley, cherry tomatoes, feta cheese, olives and parsley.
4. Finish each jar off by drizzling 1 tablespoon of olive oil and covering with a lid.

Nutritional Facts (463 g per single serving)
Calories 441
Fats 28 g
Carbs 49 g
Protein 20 g
Sodium 1291 mg

Apple and Orange Buckwheat Salad

Servings: 1

Ingredients

1 cup chicken or vegetable stock
1/3 cup raw buckwheat groats
1 small apple
1 small orange, halved, divided
1 cup cherry tomatoes
1 cup baby spinach
1/3 cup crumbled feta cheese
1 cup lentil sprouts

Dressing
1 tablespoon balsamic vinegar
1 teaspoon wholegrain mustard
2 tablespoon olive oil
Salt and pepper, to taste

Preparation

1. In a medium saucepan, bring the chicken or vegetable stock to a boil over high heat. Rinse the buckwheat groats under cold water until the water becomes clear. Add the buckwheat to the boiling water and reduce the heat to low. Cover with the lid and allow it to continue simmering for 20 minutes. Turn the heat off and drain off any excess liquid. Leave the lid on for 10 more minutes to allow the buckwheat to soak up any excess moisture.
2. Core the apple and cut it into thin slices. Squeeze the juice of half the orange over it.

3. To make the dressing: Squeeze the juice of the other half of the orange into a small bowl. Whisk in the balsamic vinegar, mustard, olive oil, and salt and pepper to taste.
4. Spoon 3 tablespoons of the dressing into a quart-sized jar and add the cooked buckwheat to it. Layer the rest of the ingredients in the following order: tomatoes, apple, spinach, cheese, and sprouts.
5. Cover with a lid and refrigerate.

Nutritional Facts (629 g per single serving)
Calories 838
Fats 41 g
Carbs 108 g
Protein 24 g
Sodium 507 mg

Mediterranean Millet Salad

Servings: 4

Ingredients
1 cup millet, rinsed
2 cups water
1 teaspoon salt
2 tablespoons olive oil
1 large tomato, chopped
1 green bell pepper, seeded and chopped
½ cup flat-leaf parsley, chopped
½ cup beets, diced
2 Kirby cucumbers, diced
1 cup olives, pitted and sliced
½ lemon, cut into wedges

Dressing
1/3 cup Greek yogurt
1/3 cup hummus
½ lemon juice
1 tablespoon water

Preparation
1. In a medium saucepan, bring the water to a boil over high heat. Add the millet and salt to and reduce the heat to low. Cover with a lid and allow it to continue simmering for 20 minutes, or until all the water has evaporated. Turn the heat off and cover with a lid for another 15 minutes.
2. To make the dressing: Whisk together all the dressing ingredients in a small bowl until well combined.

3. In a separate small bowl, toss the tomato, bell pepper, parsley and a pinch of salt together.
4. To assemble, divide the beets equally among 4 pint-sized jars. Add the cooked millet, tomato-pepper mix, cucumbers, dressing and olives.
5. Place a wedge of lemon inside each jar and cover it with a lid. Refrigerate until ready to serve.

Nutritional Facts (404 g per single serving)
Calories 412
Fats 19 g
Carbs 52 g
Protein 13 g
Sodium 871 mg

About the Author

Louise Davidson is an avid cook who likes simple flavors and easy-to-make meals. She lives in Tennessee with her husband, her three grown children, her two dogs, and the family's cat, Whiskers. She loves the outdoor and has mastered the art of camp cooking on open fires and barbecue grills.

In colder months, she loves to whip up some slow cooker meals, and uses her favorite cooking tools in her kitchen, the cast iron pans, and Dutch oven. She also is very busy preparing Christmas treats for her extended family and friends. She gets busy baking for the holiday season sometimes as early as October. Her recipes are cherished by everyone who has tasted her foods and holiday treats.

Louise is a part-time writer of cookbooks, sharing her love of food, her experience, and her family's secret recipes with her readers.

She also loves to learn and share tips and tricks to make life a breeze.

More Books from Louise Davidson

Appendix - Cooking Conversion Charts

1. Volumes

US Fluid Oz.	US	US Dry Oz.	Metric Liquid ml
¼ oz.	2 tsp.	1 oz.	10 ml.
½ oz.	1 tbsp.	2 oz.	15 ml.
1 oz.	2 tbsp.	3 oz.	30 ml.
2 oz.	¼ cup	3½ oz.	60 ml.
4 oz.	½ cup	4 oz.	125 ml.
6 oz.	¾ cup	6 oz.	175 ml.
8 oz.	1 cup	8 oz.	250 ml.

Tsp.= teaspoon - tbsp.= tablespoon – oz.= ounce – ml.= millimeter

2. Oven Temperatures

Celsius (°C)	Fahrenheit (°F)
90	220
110	225
120	250
140	275
150	300
160	325
180	350
190	375
200	400
215	425
230	450
250	475
260	500

Printed in Great Britain
by Amazon